ERNESTO LECUONA
PIANO MUSIC

D1616282

ISBN 0-7935-6982-6

EDWARD B.
MARKS MUSIC
COMPANY

EXCLUSIVELY DISTRIBUTED BY

HAL•LEONARD®
CORPORATION
7777 W. BLUEMOUND RD. P.O. BOX 13819 MILWAUKEE, WI 53213

Copyright © 1996 by HAL LEONARD CORPORATION
International Copyright Secured   All Rights Reserved

For all works contained herein:
Unauthorized copying, arranging, adapting, recording or public performance is an infringement of copyright.
Infringers are liable under the law.

Visit Hal Leonard on the internet at http://www.halleonard.com

ERNESTO LECUONA

CONTENTS

ERNESTO $\mathcal{L}$ ECUONA

ERNESTO LECUONA

ERNESTO LECUONA (1896–1963) was born in Guanabacoa, Cuba, just across the bay from Havana. As a young child he showed exceptional pianistic ability; he made his performing debut at age five. He was composing by the time he was eleven, and for much of his life, the twin pursuits of performance and composition competed for his time and energy. Eventually, he chose the latter as his primary emphasis, but not before he had established himself as a talented pianist on concert stages around the world. Similarities to one of his American contemporaries earned him the nickname "the Cuban Gershwin."

His compositions include fifty-three works for theater, twelve film scores, thirty-five orchestral works, and 176 pieces for piano. As a gifted pianist, it was only natural that he should write a great deal for his instrument. The captivating melodies and engaging rhythms of such pieces as "Malagueña," "La comparsa," and "Andalucía" have made them perennial favorites in concerts and on recordings, but such mass appeal might obscure the depth and substance of works such as "Ante el Escorial" and "San Francisco el grande."

Of Lecuona's 406 songs, many originated in his scores for stage and screen, such as "Maria-La-O" (from the *zarzuela,* or musical play, of the same title) and "Mi Vida" (from the film *Carnival in Costa Rica*). Others were independent efforts—often with the composer serving as his own lyricist—such as "Siboney." Still others were derived from his compositions for piano, as if to say that his instrumental melodies deserved to be shared with the voice. Among these are "From One Love to Another" ("Danza lucumi") and "The Breeze and I" ("Andalucía").

Lecuona's music spans a broad range of styles. As a composer, he embodied the many cultural streams that converged on his homeland—from the native Cuban ("19th Century Cuban Dances") to the ancestral Spanish ("Granada") to the African ("Danzas afro-cubanas") and even to the North American ("Tres miniaturas"). As a performer—both as a pianist and as a bandleader—he served as a cultural ambassador, figuratively and literally, for in 1943 he was appointed honorary cultural attaché at the Cuban Embassy in the United States. In his own country, he helped found the Havana Symphony and lent his assistance to many aspiring musicians.

At the time of this writing, in celebration of the 100th anniversary of the composer's birth, his entire output of piano music is being recorded by pianist Thomas Tirino and released in installments on CD by the BIS label. It is a monument to the scope of Lecuona's talent and a testament to his enduring stature as a composer.

CÓRDOBA

By ERNESTO LECUONA

Copyright © 1928 by Edward B. Marks Music Company
Copyright Renewed
International Copyright Secured   All Rights Reserved
Used by Permission

ANDALUCÍA

By ERNESTO LECUONA

Allegro Vivace

Copyright © 1928 by Edward B. Marks Music Company
Copyright Renewed
International Copyright Secured   All Rights Reserved
Used by Permission

ALHAMBRA

By ERNESTO LECUONA

Copyright © 1928 by Edward B. Marks Music Company
Copyright Renewed
International Copyright Secured   All Rights Reserved
Used by Permission

GITANERÍAS

By ERNESTO LECUONA

Copyright © 1928 by Edward B. Marks Music Company
Copyright Renewed
International Copyright Secured   All Rights Reserved
Used by Permission

GUADALQUIVIR

By ERNESTO LECUONA

Copyright © 1928 by Edward B. Marks Music Company
Copyright Renewed
International Copyright Secured   All Rights Reserved
Used by Permission

MALAGUEÑA

By ERNESTO LECUONA

Copyright © 1928 by Edward B. Marks Music Company
Copyright Renewed
International Copyright Secured   All Rights Reserved
Used by Permission

34

36

ANTE EL ESCORIAL

By ERNESTO LECUONA

Copyright © 1943, 1944 by Edward B. Marks Music Company
Copyright Renewed
International Copyright Secured   All Rights Reserved
Used by Permission

42

44

ARAGÓN

By ERNESTO LECUONA

Copyright © 1940 by Edward B. Marks Music Company
Copyright Renewed
International Copyright Secured   All Rights Reserved
Used by Permission

ARAGONESA

By ERNESTO LECUONA

Copyright © 1945, 1946 by Edward B. Marks Music Company
Copyright Renewed
International Copyright Secured   All Rights Reserved
Used by Permission

NO HABLES MÁS!!
(SPEAK NO MORE)

By ERNESTO LECUONA

Copyright © 1929 by Edward B. Marks Music Company
Copyright Renewed
International Copyright Secured   All Rights Reserved
Used by Permission

NO PUEDO CONTIGO
(I CANNOT MAKE YOU UNDERSTAND)

By ERNESTO LECUONA

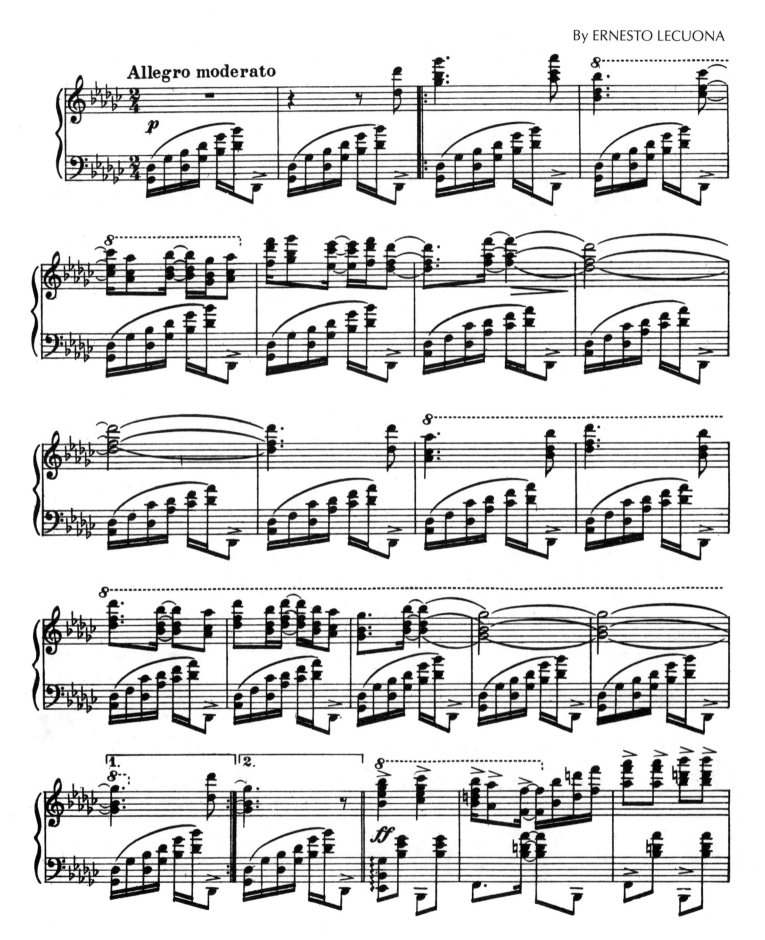

Copyright © 1929 by Edward B. Marks Music Company
Copyright Renewed
International Copyright Secured   All Rights Reserved
Used by Permission

AHÍ VIENE EL CHINO
(HERE COMES THE CHINAMAN)

By ERNESTO LECUONA

Allegro ma non troppo

Copyright © 1929 by Edward B. Marks Music Company
Copyright Renewed
International Copyright Secured   All Rights Reserved
Used by Permission

¿POR QUÉ TE VAS?
(WHY DO YOU GO)

By ERNESTO LECUONA

Copyright © 1929 by Edward B. Marks Music Company
Copyright Renewed
International Copyright Secured   All Rights Reserved
Used by Permission

LOLA ESTÁ DE FIESTA
(LOLA IS CELEBRATING)

By ERNESTO LECUONA

Copyright © 1929 by Edward B. Marks Music Company
Copyright Renewed
International Copyright Secured   All Rights Reserved
Used by Permission

Poco più mosso

EN TRES POR CUATRO
(IN THREE QUARTER TIME)

By ERNESTO LECUONA

Copyright © 1929 by Edward B. Marks Music Company
Copyright Renewed
International Copyright Secured   All Rights Reserved
Used by Permission

LA CONGA DE MEDIA NOCHE

By ERNESTO LECUONA

Copyright © 1930 by Edward B. Marks Music Company
Copyright Renewed
International Copyright Secured   All Rights Reserved
Used by Permission

DANZA NEGRA

By ERNESTO LECUONA

Copyright © 1934 by Edward B. Marks Music Company
Copyright Renewed
International Copyright Secured   All Rights Reserved
Used by Permission

90

Tempo I.

... Y LA NEGRA BAILABA!

By ERNESTO LECUONA

Copyright © 1930 by Edward B. Marks Music Company
Copyright Renewed
International Copyright Secured   All Rights Reserved
Used by Permission

95

DANZA DE LOS ÑAÑIGOS
(DANCE OF THE NEGROES)

By ERNESTO LECUONA

Copyright © 1930 by Edward B. Marks Music Company
Copyright Renewed
International Copyright Secured   All Rights Reserved
Used by Permission

97

DANZA LUCUMI

By ERNESTO LECUONA

Copyright © 1930 by Edward B. Marks Music Company
Copyright Renewed
International Copyright Secured   All Rights Reserved
Used by Permission

101

LA COMPARSA
(CARNIVAL PROCESSION)

By ERNESTO LECUONA

Copyright © 1929, 1930 by Edward B. Marks Music Company
Copyright Renewed
International Copyright Secured   All Rights Reserved
Used by Permission

CANTO DEL GUAJIRO
(SONG OF THE CUBAN FARMER)

By ERNESTO LECUONA

Copyright © 1954, 1955 by Edward B. Marks Music Company
Copyright Renewed
International Copyright Secured   All Rights Reserved
Used by Permission

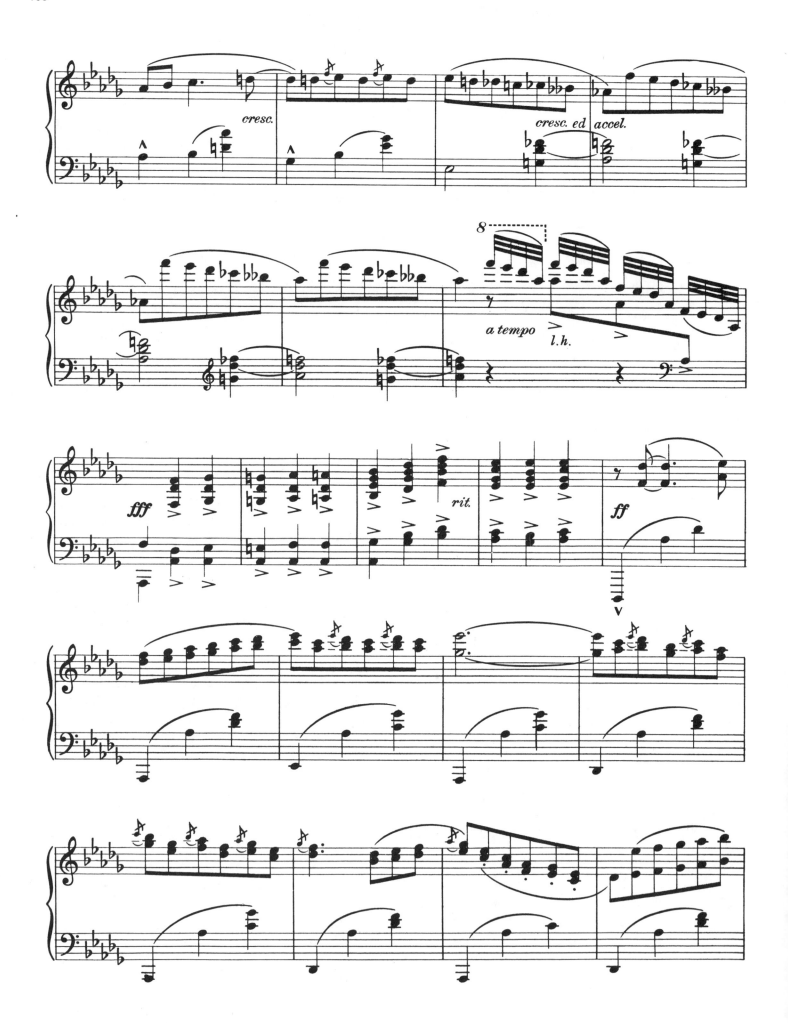

110

GOOD MORNING
(BUENOS DÍAS)

By ERNESTO LECUONA

Copyright © 1956 by Edward B. Marks Music Company
Copyright Renewed
International Copyright Secured   All Rights Reserved
Used by Permission

THE PUPPETS DANCE
(EL BAILE DE LA MUÑECA)

By ERNESTO LECUONA

Copyright © 1956 by Edward B. Marks Music Company
Copyright Renewed
International Copyright Secured   All Rights Reserved
Used by Permission

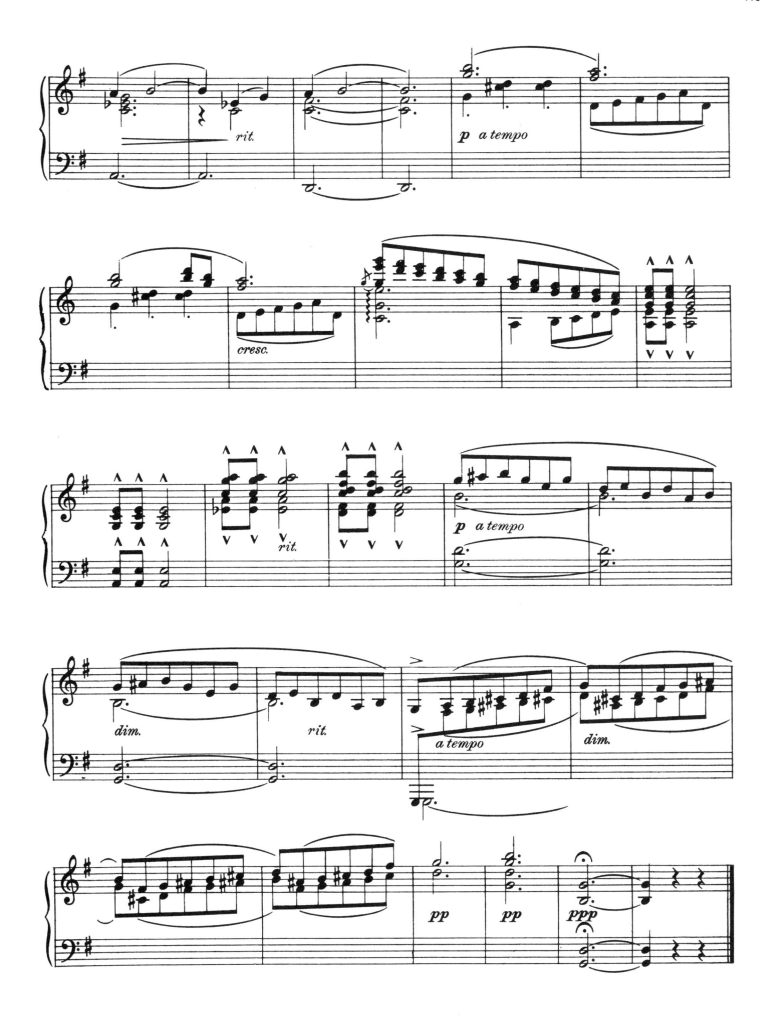

MERRY-GO-ROUND WHIRL
(CAROUSEL)

By ERNESTO LECUONA

Copyright © 1956 by Edward B. Marks Music Company
Copyright Renewed
International Copyright Secured   All Rights Reserved
Used by Permission

THE MOON LIGHTS UP
(CANCIÓN DE LUNA)

By ERNESTO LECUONA

Copyright © 1956 by Edward B. Marks Music Company
Copyright Renewed
International Copyright Secured   All Rights Reserved
Used by Permission

THE DOLLS HAVE A PARTY
(BACANAL DE MUÑECOS)

By ERNESTO LECUONA

Allegro moderato

Copyright © 1956 by Edward B. Marks Music Company
Copyright Renewed
International Copyright Secured   All Rights Reserved
Used by Permission

130

GRANADA

By ERNESTO LECUONA

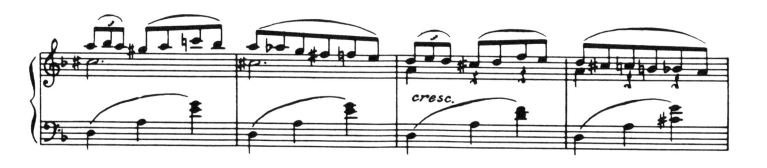

Copyright © 1946 by Edward B. Marks Music Company
Copyright Renewed
International Copyright Secured   All Rights Reserved
Used by Permission

LA PRIMERA EN LA FRENTE

By ERNESTO LECUONA

Copyright © 1943 by Edward B. Marks Music Company
Copyright Renewed
International Copyright Secured   All Rights Reserved
Used by Permission

A LA ANTIGUA

By ERNESTO LECUONA

Copyright © 1943 by Edward B. Marks Music Company
Copyright Renewed
International Copyright Secured   All Rights Reserved
Used by Permission

IMPROMPTU

By ERNESTO LECUONA

Copyright © 1943 by Edward B. Marks Music Company
Copyright Renewed
International Copyright Secured   All Rights Reserved
Used by Permission

146

INTERRUMPIDA

By ERNESTO LECUONA

Copyright © 1943 by Edward B. Marks Music Company
Copyright Renewed
International Copyright Secured   All Rights Reserved
Used by Permission

LA MULATA

By ERNESTO LECUONA

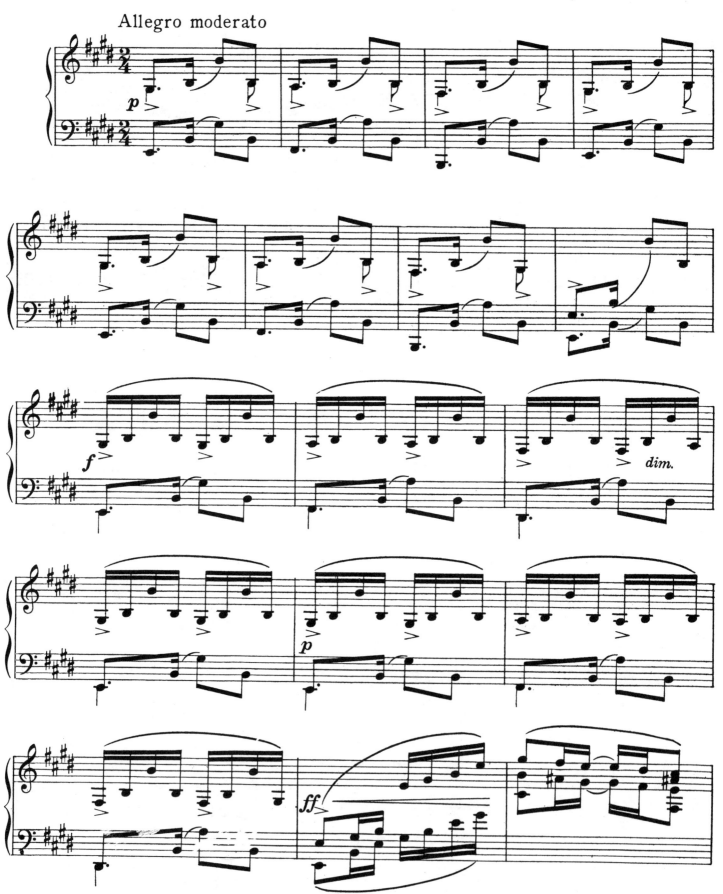

Copyright © 1943 by Edward B. Marks Music Company
Copyright Renewed
International Copyright Secured   All Rights Reserved
Used by Permission

ARABESQUE

By ERNESTO LECUONA

Copyright © 1943 by Edward B. Marks Music Company
Copyright Renewed
International Copyright Secured   All Rights Reserved
Used by Permission

Tempo I

ELLA Y YO

By ERNESTO LECUONA

Copyright © 1943 by Edward B. Marks Music Company
Copyright Renewed
International Copyright Secured   All Rights Reserved
Used by Permission

LA CARDENENSE

By ERNESTO LECUONA

Copyright © 1943 by Edward B. Marks Music Company
Copyright Renewed
International Copyright Secured   All Rights Reserved
Used by Permission

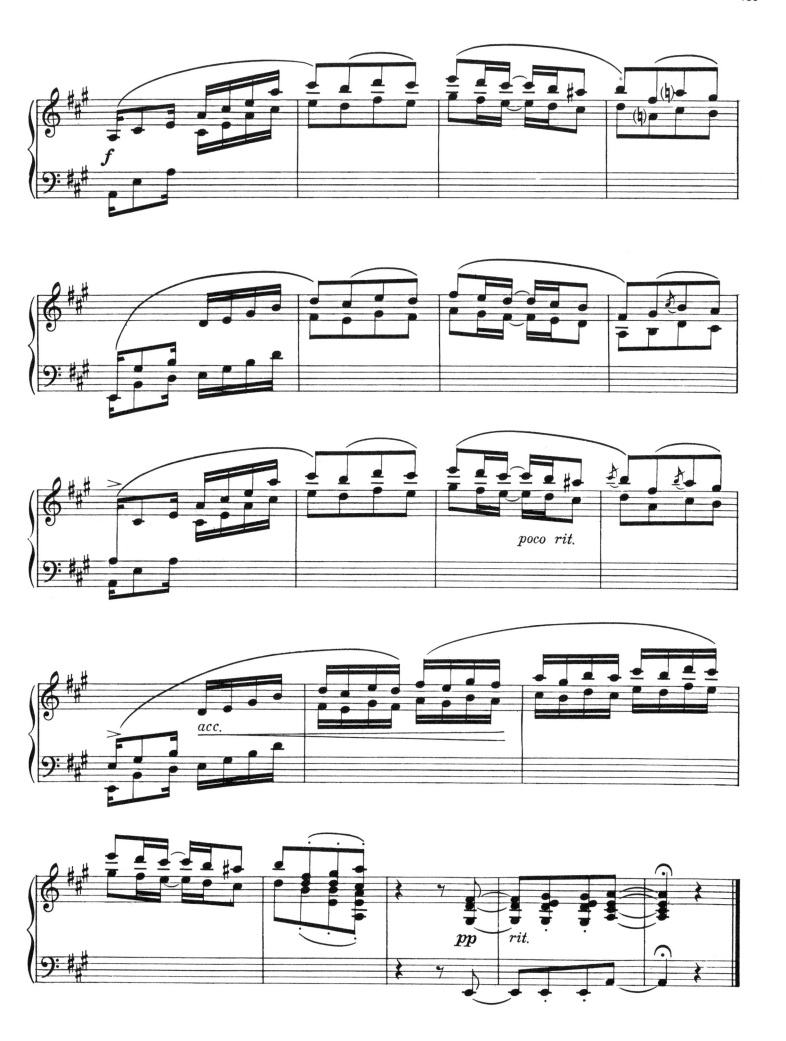

AL FIN TE VI

By ERNESTO LECUONA

Copyright © 1943 by Edward B. Marks Music Company
Copyright Renewed
International Copyright Secured   All Rights Reserved
Used by Permission

MINSTRELS

By ERNESTO LECUONA

Copyright © 1943 by Edward B. Marks Music Company
Copyright Renewed
International Copyright Secured   All Rights Reserved
Used by Permission

MAZURKA GLISSANDO

By ERNESTO LECUONA

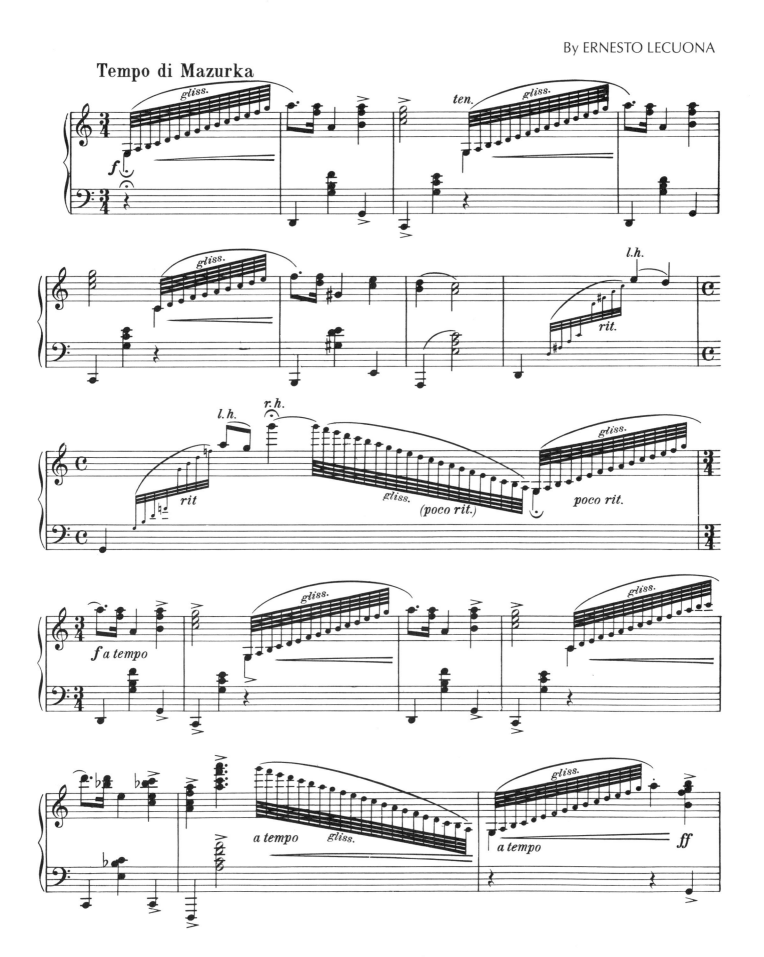

Copyright © 1940 by Edward B. Marks Music Company
Copyright Renewed
International Copyright Secured   All Rights Reserved
Used by Permission

SAN FRANCISCO EL GRANDE

By ERNESTO LECUONA

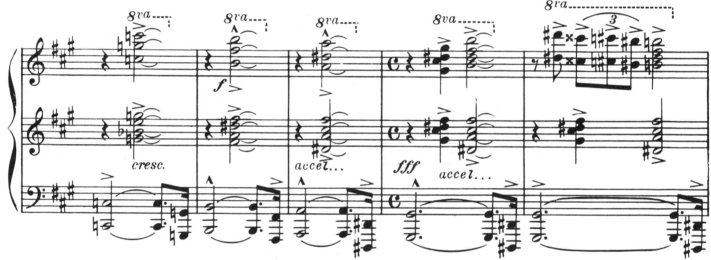

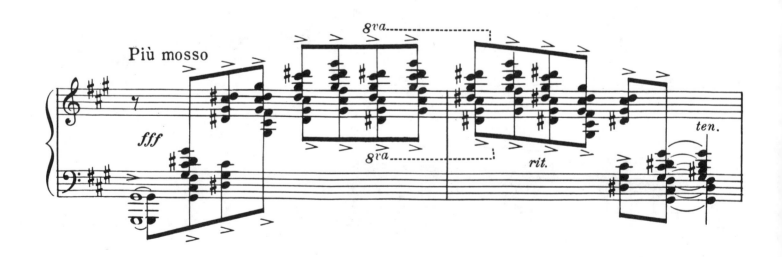

Copyright © 1943, 1944 by Edward B. Marks Music Company
Copyright Renewed
International Copyright Secured   All Rights Reserved
Used by Permission

170

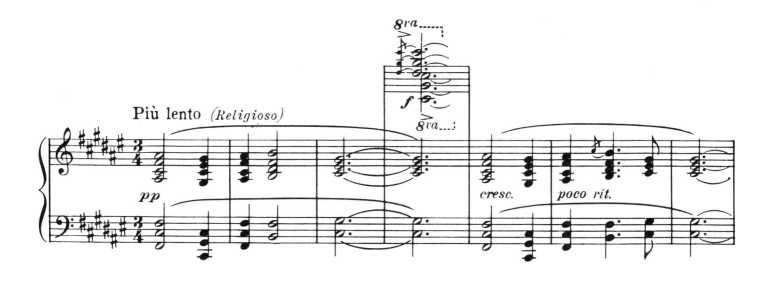

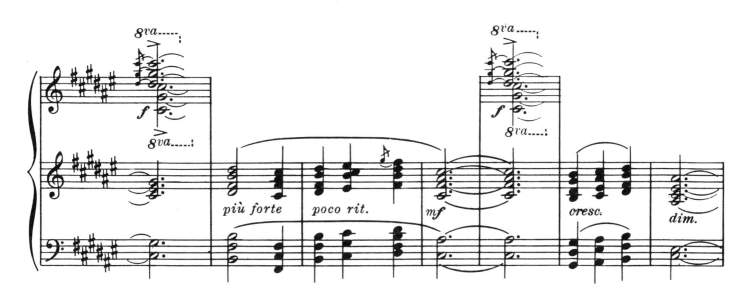

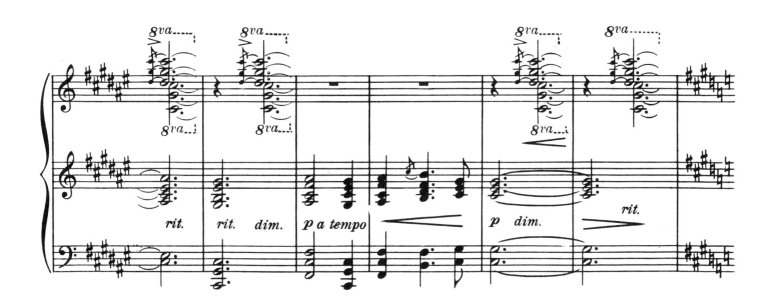

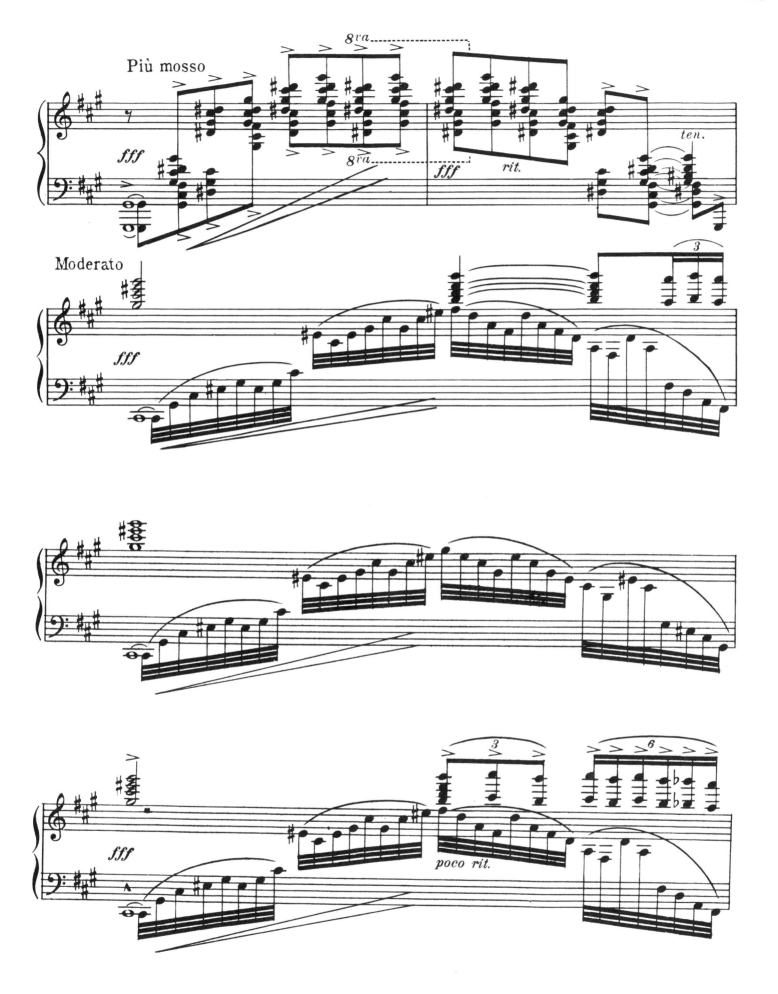

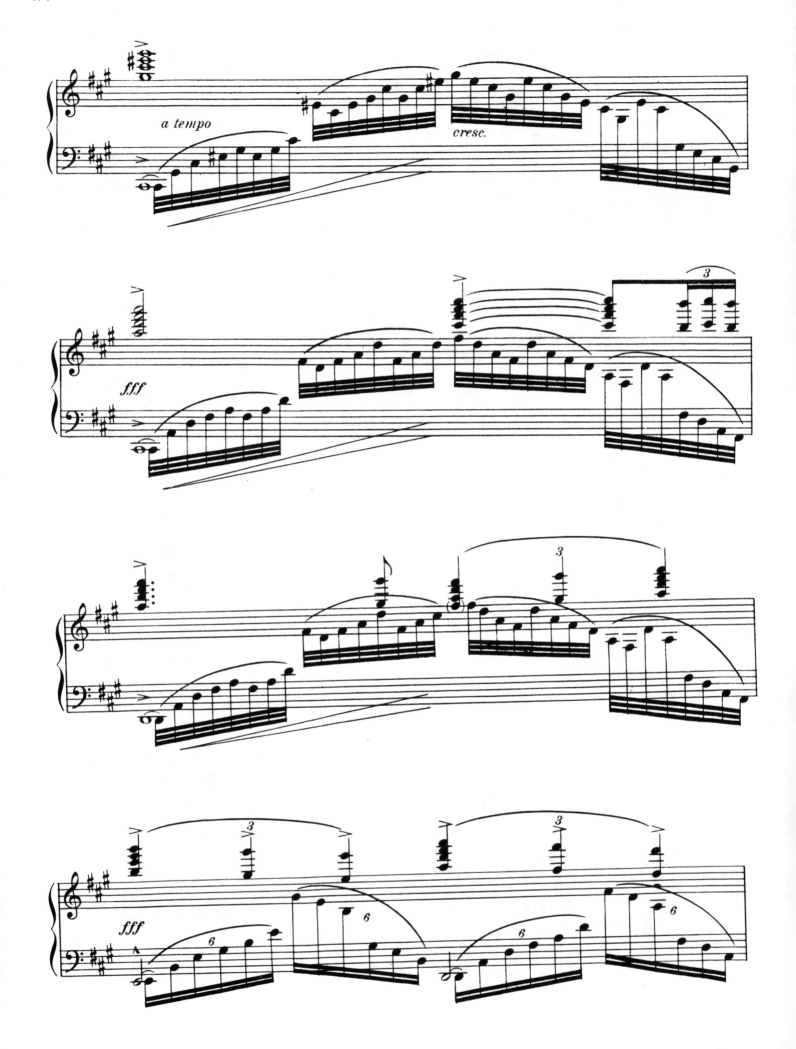

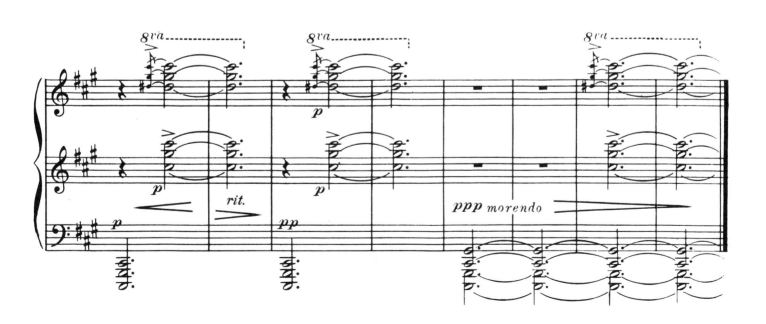

BELL-FLOWER

By ERNESTO LECUONA

Copyright © 1943 by Edward B. Marks Music Company
Copyright Renewed
International Copyright Secured   All Rights Reserved
Used by Permission

MUSIC BOX

By ERNESTO LECUONA

Copyright © 1943 by Edward B. Marks Music Company
Copyright Renewed
International Copyright Secured   All Rights Reserved
Used by Permission

POLICHINELA

By ERNESTO LECUONA

Copyright © 1943 by Edward B. Marks Music Company
Copyright Renewed
International Copyright Secured   All Rights Reserved
Used by Permission

ZAMBRA GITANA

By ERNESTO LECUONA

Copyright © 1944, 1945, 1946 by Edward B. Marks Music Company
Copyright Renewed
International Copyright Secured   All Rights Reserved
Used by Permission

Franz
metronome